HISTORY

How to Use Your SD-X Reader with This Book

In this series, you can explore Britannica content in an interactive format. You can read the book and study the photographs and illustrations, and a touch of the SD-X Reader adds in-depth audio information, word definitions, and learning games.

1. Press the Power button to turn the SD-X Reader on or off. The LED will light up when the SD-X Reader is on.

2. Touch the volume buttons found on this page or on the Table of Contents page to adjust the volume.

3. Touch photographs and illustrations with the SD-X Reader to hear additional information. In a block of text, touch words that are a different color or size to hear a definition or more information.

4. As you touch around the page, you'll encounter games and quizzes. Touch the header or image that started the game to stop playing the game.

5. After two minutes of inactivity, the Reader will beep and go to sleep.

6. If the batteries are low, the Reader will beep twice and the LED will start blinking. Replace the batteries by following the instructions on the next page. The SD-X Reader uses two AAA batteries.

7. To use headphones or earbuds, plug them into the headphone jack on the bottom of the SD-X Reader.

CHANGE THE VOLUME WITH THESE BUTTONS

UP   DOWN

Battery Information
Interactive Pen includes 2 replaceable AAA batteries (UM-4 or LR03).

Battery Installation
1. Open battery door with small flat-head or Phillips screwdriver.
2. Install new batteries according to +/- polarity. If batteries are not installed properly, the device will not function.
3. Replace battery door; secure with small screw.

Battery Safety
Batteries must be replaced by adults only. Properly dispose of used batteries. Do not dispose of batteries in fire; batteries may explode or leak. See battery manufacturer for disposal recommendations. Do not mix alkaline, standard (carbon-zinc), or rechargeable (nickel-cadmium) batteries. Do not mix old and new batteries. Only recommended batteries of the same or equivalent type should be used. Remove weakened or dead batteries. Never short-circuit the supply terminals. Non-rechargeable batteries are not to be recharged. Do not use rechargeable batteries. If batteries are swallowed, in the USA, promptly see a doctor and have the doctor phone 1-202-625-3333 collect. In other countries, have the doctor call your local poison control center. Batteries should be changed when sounds mix, distort, or become otherwise unintelligible as batteries weaken. The electrostatic discharge may interfere with the sound module. If this occurs, please simply restart the product.

In Europe, the dustbin symbol indicates that batteries, rechargeable batteries, button cells, battery packs, and similar materials must not be discarded in household waste. Batteries containing hazardous substances are harmful to the environment and to health. Please help to protect the environment from health risks by telling your children to dispose of batteries properly and by taking batteries to local collection points. Batteries handled in this manner are safely recycled.

Warning: Changes or modifications to this unit not expressly approved by the party responsible for compliance could void the user's authority to operate the equipment.

NOTE: This equipment has been tested and found to comply with the limits for a Class B digital device, pursuant to Part 15 of the FCC Rules. These limits are designed to provide reasonable protection against harmful interference in a residential installation. This equipment generates, uses, and can radiate radio frequency energy and, if not installed and used in accordance with the instructions, may cause harmful interference to radio communications. However, there is no guarantee that interference will not occur in a particular installation. If this equipment does cause harmful interference to radio or television reception, which can be determined by turning the equipment off and on, the user is encouraged to try to correct the interference by one or more of the following measures: Reorient or relocate the receiving antenna. Increase the separation between the equipment and receiver. Connect the equipment into an outlet on a circuit different from that to which the receiver is connected. Consult the dealer or an experienced radio TV technician for help.

Cover art from Shutterstock.com.

Interior art from Encyclopædia Britannica, Inc.; Getty Images; and Shutterstock.com. Page 56–59 art from NASA; NASA/JPL; NASA/JPL/Space Science Institute; S. Molau and P. Jenniskens, NASA Ames Research Center; NASA, ESA, J. Parker, P. Thomas, L. McFadden, and M. Mutchler and Z. Levay.

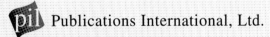 Publications International, Ltd.

Customer Service
customer_service@pubint.com

ISBN: 978-1-4508-8411-2

Manufactured in China.

8 7 6 5 4 3 2 1

CONTENTS

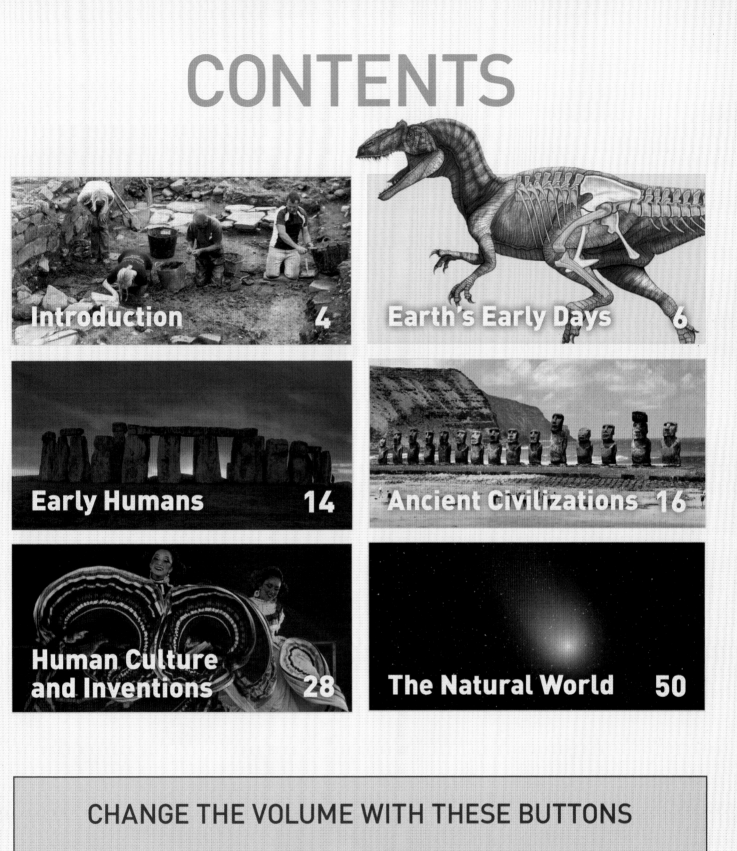

CHANGE THE VOLUME WITH THESE BUTTONS

UP   DOWN

INTRODUCTION

When did amphibians first appear on Earth? What were the early dinosaurs like? Why did humans first begin to build cities? What did people wear in ancient Greece? Where was the first skyscraper built? When did people first use shoes, play volleyball, and exchange money? How do carnivorous plants trap bugs? The answers to these questions—and a lot more information—can be found in this book. As you read, you'll take a journey of discovery throughout time and around the globe—and beyond!

How big were the biggest dinosaurs?

In the first section of this book, take a look at what Earth was like before people.

When did humans begin to farm?

When you read "Early humans" and "Ancient civilizations," you'll learn about what life was like in ancient times.

Were the bagpipes developed in Scotland?

In "Human culture and inventions," you'll add to your knowledge of architecture, religion, music, sports, money, and inventions—both past and present!

How many spacecraft have visited Neptune?

In "The natural world," you'll look at the world around us, from plants to planets.

How do we know what happened when?

Information about the world is gathered and studied by paleontologists, archaeologists, anthropologists, historians, scientists, and others!

Paleontology is the study of prehistoric life that involves the analysis of plant and animal fossils—including those of microscopic size—preserved in rocks.

Archaeology is the scientific study of the material remains of humankind's past. Its discoveries are the principal source of knowledge about prehistoric cultures. The materials of archaeological study are both the things made by people and the things used by them.

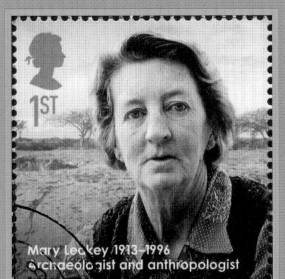

Mary Leakey 1913–1996
Archaeologist and anthropologist

The science of the origins and development of human beings and their cultures is called anthropology. Anthropologists investigate the whole range of human development and behavior, including biological variation, geographic distribution, evolutionary history, cultural history, and social relationships.

A PREHISTORIC TIMELINE

Most scientists believe that the first living organism on Earth probably evolved within a billion years of Earth's formation, which occurred roughly 4.5 billion years ago. Fossil remains of microorganisms were discovered embedded in rocks that were roughly 3.5 billion years old. While some prehistoric animals died out completely, becoming extinct, the descendants of others are still living on Earth.

Geologic time scale, 650 million years ago to the present

millions of years ago	era	period	events
0			
2.6	Cenozoic	Quaternary	evolution of humans
		Neogene	mammals diversify
50		Paleogene	
			extinction of dinosaurs
100	Mesozoic	Cretaceous	first primates
			first flowering plants
150			first birds
		Jurassic	dinosaurs diversify
200			first mammals
		Triassic	first dinosaurs
250			major extinctions
		Permian	
300	Paleozoic		reptiles diversify
	Carbon-iferous	Pennsylvanian	first reptiles scale trees seed ferns
350		Mississippian	
			first amphibians
400		Devonian	jawed fishes diversify
450		Silurian	first vascular land plants
		Ordovician	sudden diversification of metazoan families
500		Cambrian	first fishes
			first chordates
550	Late Proterozoic		first skeletal elements first soft-bodied metazoans first animal traces
600			
650			

The oldest known animal fossils are about 700 million years old; these fossils were largely impressions (molds or casts) of soft-bodied marine animals similar to modern-day jellyfish, soft corals, sea anemones, and annelid worms.

A salamander today

The first amphibians probably looked like salamanders, 3 to 4 feet (0.9 to 1.2 meters) in length, with sharp teeth and wide heads.

How big were cockroaches during the Carboniferous period?

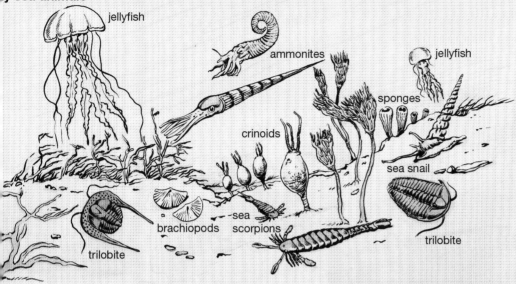

...ly sea animals

jellyfish
ammonites
jellyfish
sponges
crinoids
sea snail
brachiopods
sea scorpions
trilobite
trilobite

...als are not necessarily drawn to same scale.

© 2010 Encyclopædia Britannica, Inc.

◀ The earliest fossils date from about 570 million years ago. In those days, shallow seas covered many places that have since become dry land.

The lungfish is thought to represent a transitional stage between the fish and the amphibian. Lungfish have real lungs, which means that they can rise to the water surface to breathe.

How many species of living things are there on the Earth today?

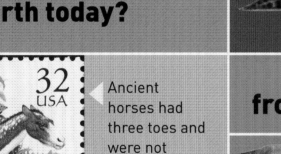

...hippus
32 USA

◀ Ancient horses had three toes and were not much larger than sheep.

Did mammals evolve from reptiles or amphibians?

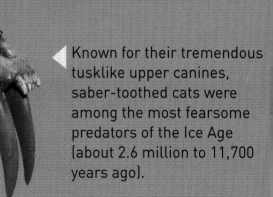

◀ Known for their tremendous tusklike upper canines, saber-toothed cats were among the most fearsome predators of the Ice Age (about 2.6 million to 11,700 years ago).

True or False?
T   F

...wo million years ago, during the Pleistocene ...poch, an immense beast with long, shaggy ...air and huge, curved tusks lumbered around ...what are now Africa, Eurasia, and North ...merica. This animal, the mammoth, was the ...ncestor of the modern elephant. Mastodons, ...imilar in appearance to mammoths, were ...arly distant relatives of the mammoths.

Mastodon   Mammoth   Elephant

DINOSAURS

For about 150 million years the predominant land animals on Earth were the dinosaurs, all of which were very different from any of the land animals known today. Dinosaurs shared numerous features with modern reptiles. Many dinosaurs walked upright like modern birds and several mammals; some walked on all fours like lizards and crocodiles.

More than 1,000 different sites containing dinosaur fossils have been uncovered around the world.

ARCTIC OCEAN
Arctic Circle
NORTH AMERICA
ASIA
EUROPE
Tropic of Cancer
PACIFIC OCEAN
PACIFIC
ATLANTIC OCEAN
AFRICA
0
SOUTH AMERICA
INDIAN OCEAN
AUSTRALIA
Antarctic Circle

• Major Dinosaur Fossil Sites

Tertiary

66.4 million years ago
Parasaurolophus
Shantungosaurus
Lambeosaurus
Tyrannosaurus
Triceratops

Late Cretaceous

97.5 million years ago
Euoplocephalus
Ornithomimus
Troodon
Protoceratops
Pachycephalosaurus
Oviraptor
Velociraptor

Early Cretaceous

144 million years ago
Hypsilophodon
Iguanodon
Psittacosaurus
Deinonychus
Brachiosaurus

Jurassic

208 million years ago
Apatosaurus
Allosaurus
Ceratosaurus
Lesothosaurus
Compsognathus
Stegosaurus
Archaeopteryx

Triassic

245 million years ago
Plateosaurus
Herrerasaurus
Coelophysis
Eoraptor

1 metre
3 feet

Are any dinosaurs alive today?

Was *Archaeopteryx* a bird or a dinosaur? ▶

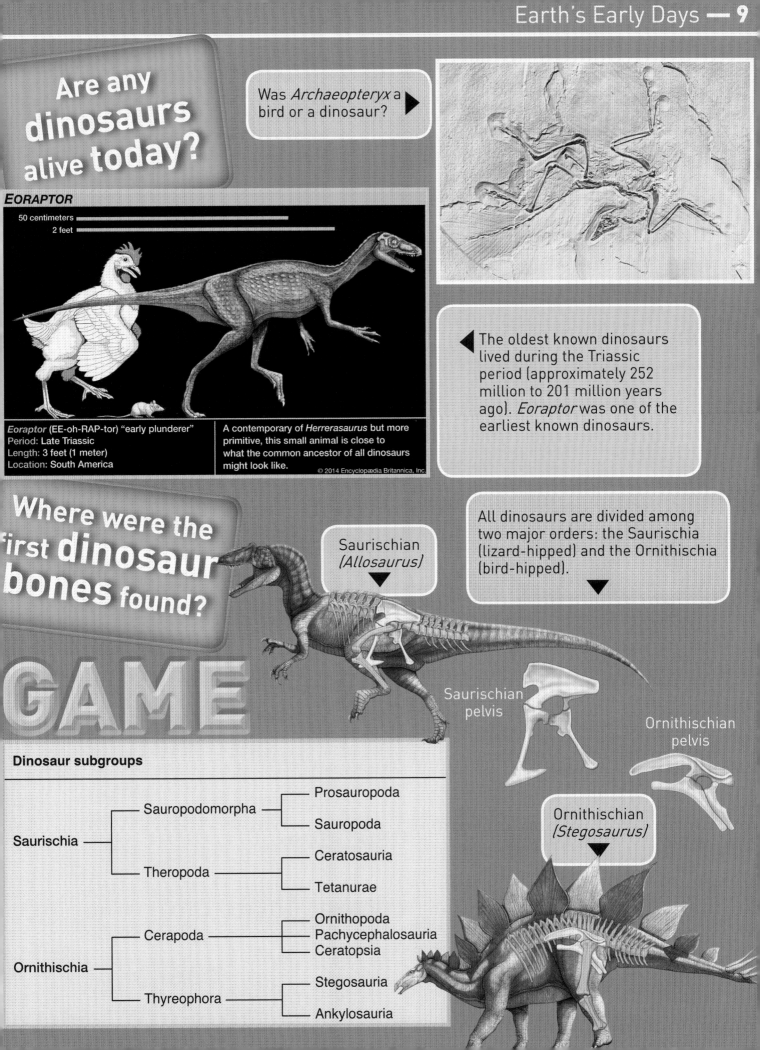

EORAPTOR

50 centimeters
2 feet

Eoraptor (EE-oh-RAP-tor) "early plunderer"
Period: Late Triassic
Length: 3 feet (1 meter)
Location: South America

A contemporary of *Herrerasaurus* but more primitive, this small animal is close to what the common ancestor of all dinosaurs might look like.

© 2014 Encyclopædia Britannica, Inc.

◀ The oldest known dinosaurs lived during the Triassic period (approximately 252 million to 201 million years ago). *Eoraptor* was one of the earliest known dinosaurs.

Where were the first dinosaur bones found?

GAME

All dinosaurs are divided among two major orders: the Saurischia (lizard-hipped) and the Ornithischia (bird-hipped). ▼

Saurischian
(*Allosaurus*)
▼

Saurischian pelvis

Ornithischian pelvis

Ornithischian
(*Stegosaurus*)
▼

Dinosaur subgroups

- Saurischia
  - Sauropodomorpha
    - Prosauropoda
    - Sauropoda
  - Theropoda
    - Ceratosauria
    - Tetanurae
- Ornithischia
  - Cerapoda
    - Ornithopoda
    - Pachycephalosauria
    - Ceratopsia
  - Thyreophora
    - Stegosauria
    - Ankylosauria

THE MEAT EATERS

HERRERASAURUS

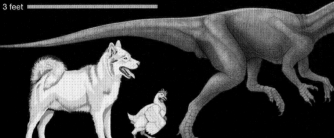

1 meter
3 feet

Herrerasaurus (eh-RAY-rah-SORE-us)
"Herrera's lizard"
Period: Late Triassic
Length: 10 feet (3 meters)
Location: South America

One of the earliest known dinosaurs, it was an agile predator with strong, clawed hands for grasping prey.

© 2010 Encyclopædia Britannica, Inc.

◄ *Herrerasaurus* is named after Victorino Herrera, who found the first specimen in 1958 near San Juan, Argentina.

COELOPHYSIS

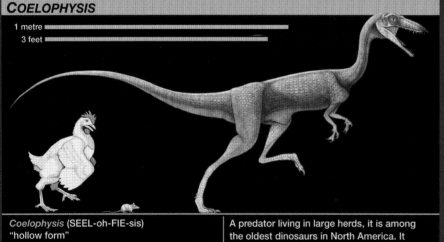

1 metre
3 feet

Coelophysis (SEEL-oh-FIE-sis)
"hollow form"
Period: Late Triassic
Length: 6 to 8 feet (about 2 metres)
Location: North America

A predator living in large herds, it is among the oldest dinosaurs in North America. It had hollow limbs, a feature similar to birds.

© 2010 Encyclopædia Britannica, Inc.

◄ *Coelophysis* fossils were first discovered in New Mexico in 1881. Later quarrying operations at Ghost Ranch in New Mexico yielded the remains of several hundred individuals of varying sizes.

COMPSOGNATHUS

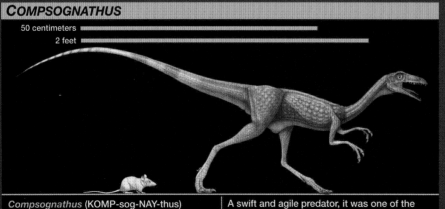

50 centimeters
2 feet

Compsognathus (KOMP-sog-NAY-thus)
"elegant jaw"
Period: Late Jurassic
Length: 2 to 3 feet (60 to 90 centimeters)
Location: Europe

A swift and agile predator, it was one of the smallest known dinosaurs.

© 2013 Encyclopædia Britannica, Inc.

◄ The first fossil evidence of *Compsognathus* was an essentially complete skeleton discovered in Bavaria in southern Germany in the late 1850s.

WHICH DINOSAUR?

A broken tailbone found in early 1869 in Grand County, Colorado, in the United States was the first fossil evidence of *Allosaurus*. When more fossils were discovered in Colorado in 1877, the genus *Allosaurus*, which comes from the Latin words meaning "different lizard," was established.

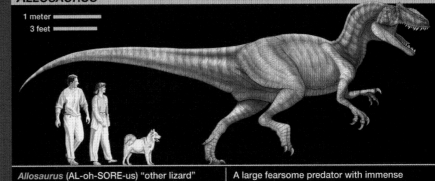

ALLOSAURUS

1 meter
3 feet

Allosaurus (AL-oh-SORE-us) "other lizard"
Period: **Late Jurassic**
Length: **25 to 35 feet (7.5 to 10.5 meters)**
Location: **North America, Africa, Australia**

A large fearsome predator with immense muscular jaws and long, serrated teeth for eating flesh.

© 2010 Encyclopædia Britannica, Inc.

The first fossil evidence of *Deinonychus* was collected over a two-year period beginning in 1964 at a site in southern Montana in the United States.

DEINONYCHUS

1 meter
3 feet

Deinonychus (die-NON-i-kus)
"terrible claw"
Period: **Early Cretaceous**
Length: **8 feet (2.5 meters), perhaps larger**
Location: **North America**

A formidable predator capable of deadly attacks. Its second toes were equipped with huge, sharp claws.

© 2010 Encyclopædia Britannica, Inc.

The first fossil evidence of *Oviraptor* was collected in 1923 at a site in Omnogov in southern Mongolia.

OVIRAPTOR

50 centimeters
2 feet

Oviraptor (OH-vih-RAP-tor) "egg thief"
Period: **Late Cretaceous**
Length: **6 feet (1.8 meters)**
Location: **Asia, North America**

A birdlike predator or omnivore with a crest above its snout and a horny beak.

© 2010 Encyclopædia Britannica, Inc.

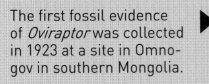

THE PLANT EATERS

LESOTHOSAURUS

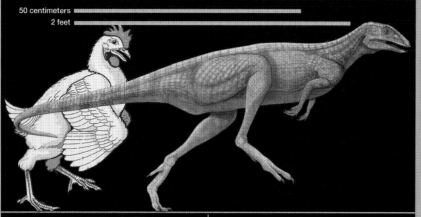

50 centimeters
2 feet

Lesothosaurus (le-SOO-too-SORE-us)
"Lesotho lizard"
Period: **Early Jurassic**
Length: **3.3 feet (1 meter)**
Location: **Africa, South America**

This tiny herbivore was lightly built because of some of its hollow bones.

© 2010 Encyclopædia Britannica, Inc.

◀ The first definitive fossil evidence from *Lesothosaurus*, consisting of at least four skulls and other skeletal pieces, was described in 1978. It was named after the site of its discovery—the Upper Elliot Formation in the Mafeteng district of Lesotho in southern Africa.

STEGOSAURUS

1 meter
3 feet

Stegosaurus (STEG-oh-SORE-us)
"roof lizard"
Period: **Late Jurassic**
Length: **30 feet (9 meters)**
Location: **North America**

The largest known plated dinosaur, this herbivore had two rows of tall bony plates running along its back.

© 2010 Encyclopædia Britannica, Inc.

◀ Fossil evidence of *Stegosaurus* has been discovered in the western region of the United States, particularly in the states of Colorado, Wyoming, Utah, and Oklahoma. Colorado has adopted *Stegosaurus* as its state fossil.

APATOSAURUS

1 meter
3 feet

Apatosaurus (formerly *Brontosaurus*)
(ah-PAT-oh-SORE-us) "deceptive lizard"
Period: **Late Jurassic and Early Cretaceous**
Length: **70 feet (21 metres)**
Height: **19 feet (5.8 meters)**
Location: **North America, Europe**

This massive herbivore weighed as much as five adult elephants. Its long whiplash tail helped balance it when it walked.

© 2010 Encyclopædia Britannica, Inc.

◀ The first fossil evidence of *Apatosaurus*, a hipbone, was collected in 1877 in the United States near Morrison, Colorado. Most *Apatosaurus* fossils have been found at the Morrison Formation in Wyoming, Utah, Oklahoma, and Colorado.

True or False?   T   F

The first fossil evidence of *Hypsilophodon* was discovered on the Isle of Wight in the mid–19th century. *Hypsilophodon* was initially thought to be a tree dweller. A reassessment of the evidence, however, led paleontologists to conclude that *Hypsilophodon* lived on the ground.

HYPSILOPHODON

1 meter
3 feet

Hypsilophodon (HIP-sih-LOH-foh-don)
"high ridge tooth"
Period: Early Cretaceous
Length: 6.5 feet (2 meters)
Location: Europe, North America

Small and fast, this herbivore had self-sharpening cheek teeth and cheek pouches for storing food.

© 2010 Encyclopædia Britannica, Inc.

The first fossil evidence of *Protoceratops* was discovered in Mongolia in the 1920s.

PROTOCERATOPS

1 meter
3 feet

Protoceratops (PROH-toh-SERRA-tops)
"first horned face"
Period: Late Cretaceous
Length: 6 feet (1.8 meters)
Location: Asia

Solidly built, this herbivore had a parrotlike beak and bony frill.

© 2010 Encyclopædia Britannica, Inc.

Fossil skull material from *Pachycephalosaurus* has been recovered from sites in the Canadian province of Alberta and in Wyoming, South Dakota, and Montana in the United States.

PACHYCEPHALOSAURUS

1 meter
3 feet

Pachycephalosaurus
(PAK-ee-SEF-a-loh-SORE-us)
"thick-headed lizard"
Period: Late Cretaceous
Length: 15 feet (4.6 meters)
Location: North America

An herbivore with a distinctive, thick, dome-shaped skull and a low spiky snout.

© 2010 Encyclopædia Britannica, Inc.

THE STONE, BRONZE, AND IRON AGES

Scientists studying the history of early humans define several different stages in the development of culture and technology. At the stage called the Stone Age, prehistoric humans made tools out of stone. The Stone Age was not one specific time period, as different cultures in different parts of the world reached this stage at different points. It was followed in many places by two stages in which people fashioned tools of metal: the Bronze Age and the Iron Age.

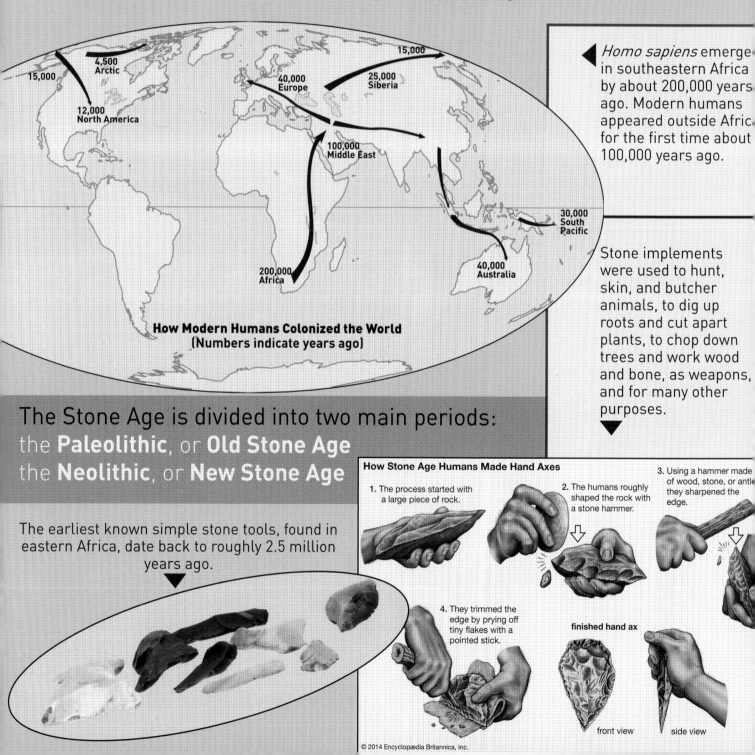

15,000

4,500
Arctic

15,000

12,000
North America

40,000
Europe

25,000
Siberia

100,000
Middle East

30,000
South
Pacific

200,000
Africa

40,000
Australia

How Modern Humans Colonized the World
(Numbers indicate years ago)

◀ *Homo sapiens* emerge in southeastern Africa by about 200,000 years ago. Modern humans appeared outside Africa for the first time about 100,000 years ago.

Stone implements were used to hunt, skin, and butcher animals, to dig up roots and cut apart plants, to chop down trees and work wood and bone, as weapons, and for many other purposes. ▼

The Stone Age is divided into two main periods:
the **Paleolithic**, or **Old Stone Age**
the **Neolithic**, or **New Stone Age**

The earliest known simple stone tools, found in eastern Africa, date back to roughly 2.5 million years ago. ▼

How Stone Age Humans Made Hand Axes

1. The process started with a large piece of rock.

2. The humans roughly shaped the rock with a stone hammer.

3. Using a hammer made of wood, stone, or antler, they sharpened the edge.

4. They trimmed the edge by prying off tiny flakes with a pointed stick.

finished hand ax

front view   side view

© 2014 Encyclopædia Britannica, Inc.

The oldest drawings of which there is any record are those on the walls of caves in which Stone Age people lived.

The prehistoric monument known as Stonehenge includes a circular arrangement of massive, upright stones surrounded by a large circular earthen embankment.

In China, people during the Shang Dynasty (1600? BC-1046 BC) used bronze to make weapons, daily tools, and elaborately decorated sacrificial vessels.

Which Age?

Stone Age (Paleolithic)

Stone Age (Neolithic)

Bronze Age

Iron Age

This picture shows the excavation site of a Bronze Age settlement in Greece. During the stage in human history called the Bronze Age, people first began to use bronze to make tools, weapons, armor, and other implements. The Bronze Age began in Greece before 3000 BC.

The stage in human cultural and technological development called the Iron Age is characterized by the **smelting** of iron and its widespread use in tools. The Iron Age is usually considered to have begun in the Middle East and southeastern Europe in about 1200 to 1000 BC, when iron tools came into wide use.

THE FIRST CIVILIZATIONS

All of the major ancient civilizations—in Mesopotamia, Egypt, the Indus valley, and China—emerged in the 4th millennium BC. Historians still debate over which one emerged first. It may well have been in the Middle East, in an area called the Fertile Crescent.

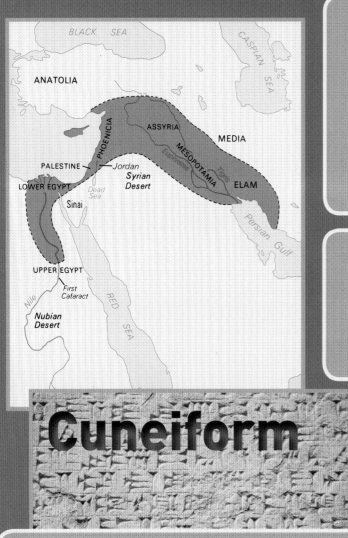

How Civilizations Developed

agriculture
goods and pottery
buildings
mathematics
writing

The Fertile Crescent stretches from the Nile River in Egypt northward along the coast of the historical region of Palestine, then eastward into Asia to include Mesopotamia. In this area people settled along the riverbanks and practiced field agriculture.

Cuneiform

Ziggurat

By about 5000 BC, small tribes of farmers had made their way to the river valleys of **Mesopotamia**. On the floodplains they raised wheat, barley, and peas. They cut through the riverbanks so that water for their crops could flow to lower lying soil. These early irrigation systems were more fully developed by the Sumerians, who drained marshes and dug canals, dikes, and ditches. The need for cooperation on these large irrigation projects led to the growth of government and law.

TRUE or False?

T   F

Archaeologists have discovered a 5,000-year-old backgammon board at the site of the ancient Sumerian town of Ur.

This black column is inscribed with the Code of Hammurabi, a Babylonian king.

The Sumerians were conquered by their neighbors. But their civilization was carried on by their successors—the Akkadians, Babylonians, Assyrians, and Chaldeans. The Babylonians added to the knowledge of astronomy, advanced the knowledge of mathematics, and built the first great capital city, Babylon.

The archaeological record suggests that humans began settling in the region west of the Indus River at the Pakistan-Iran border as early as 8000 BC. The earliest known urban culture of the Indian subcontinent existed in the Indus valley from about 2500 BC to about 1700 BC.

Remnants of a city wall in what is now Zhengzhou ▼

The Indus Valley civilization grew this crop. What is it?

Although historians are not certain exactly when the Shang ruled, the dynasty is thought to have begun about 1600 BC and ended in 1046 BC. The Shang created one of the earliest advanced civilizations in East Asia.

ANCIENT EGYPT

No other country has such a long unbroken history as Egypt. Some 5,000 years ago, the Egyptians had already reached a high stage of civilization. They lived under an orderly government; they carried on commerce in ships; they built great stone structures; and, most important of all, they had acquired the art of writing.

The dynasties of Egypt:

the Old Kingdom
the Middle Kingdom
the New Kingdom
the Late Period

▲
What is this plant and why was it important in Egypt?

▲
The ancient Egyptians had three different ways of writing. They are called **hieroglyphic**, **hieratic**, and **demotic**.

◀ **A mud brick house**

◀ Villages and towns were situated near the Nile because it was the chief highway as well as the only source of water. Even the rich lived in houses of mud brick.

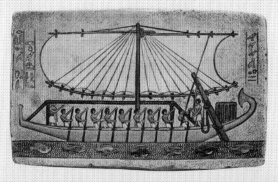

 Shipbuilders made Nile vessels with curving hulls and tall sails and cargo ships to sail to foreign lands.

◄ Construction of one of the most colossal temples of all time, the Temple of Amon at Karnak, was begun under the pharaohs of the Middle Kingdom.

How did people wear their hair in ancient Egypt?

Egyptian Beliefs START

ANCIENT GREECE

In ancient times, Greece was not a country in the modern sense but a collection of several hundred independent cities, each with its surrounding countryside. Since these cities were independent political units, they are known as city-states. In Greek, the word for city-state is *polis*, and the English word politics comes from it.

The city-state was made possible by Mediterranean geography. Because of the mountainous and coastal landscape, every little fishing village had to be able to defend itself against attack from land or sea, because outside help could not reach it easily.

Athens was a city-state in which the arts, philosophy, and democracy flourished. It attracted those who wanted to work, speak, and think in an environment of freedom. In Athens were born ideas about human nature and political society that are fundamental to the Western world today.

Plato and Socrates

The Theater of Dionysus in Athens

Ancient Greece was the birthplace of the drama of the Western world. By the 5th century BC dramas were presented at Greek religious festivals twice a year. These grew out of the worship of Dionysus.

Altogether there were more than 200 Greek dances designed for every mood and purpose. There were comic pieces, warlike works, and dances for athletes, spectacles, and religious worship.

Terpsichore, the Muse of dancing and choral song

In the religion and mythology of ancient Greece and Rome, the Muses were a group of sister goddesses who were the patrons of the arts.

What was the agora?
**a type of plow
a constellation
the marketplace
the athletic field**

Ancient Greek sculptures were:
**white
gray
painted**

What was the chiton?
**a type of insect
a type of poem
a type of garment
a type of building**

Leonidas, king of Sparta

In the 5th century BC the vast Persian Empire attempted to conquer Greece. If the Persians had succeeded, they would have set up local tyrants, called satraps, to rule Greece and would have crushed the first stirrings of democracy in Europe. The survival of Greek culture and political ideals depended on the ability of the small, disunited Greek city-states to band together and defend themselves against Persia's overwhelming strength.

Myths and Stories

Orion and Artemis

Perseus and Medusa

Odysseus and Penelope

ANCIENT ROME

The ancient city of Rome was the center of one of the largest and most powerful empires the world has ever seen. The Roman Empire was based in what is now Italy. As the Roman Empire took over more land and peoples, its influence spread throughout western Europe and into all the lands around the Mediterranean Sea.

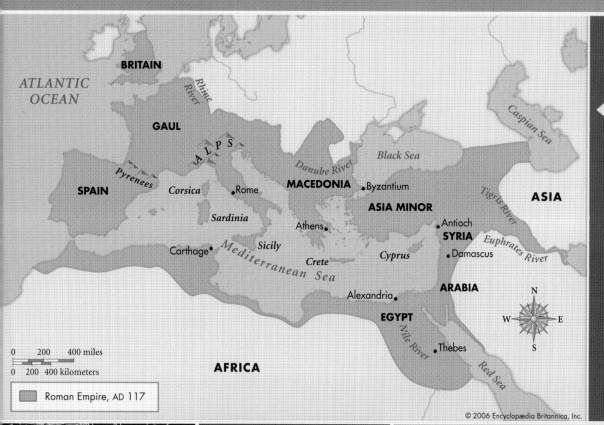

© 2006 Encyclopædia Britannica, Inc.

◀ The Roman Empire's frontiers expanded all the way to Britain and the Arabian Peninsula. The Romans built roads, bridges, and aqueducts, or water pipes, throughout their vast empire.

◀ The ancient Romans created many designs called mosaics out of tiny tiles.

How did the Romans get their news? ▶

▲ Ancient Rome was built on the swiftly flowing Tiber River. The Romans called it Father Tiber.

The Roman citizen wore a toga over his tunic. The toga was a semicircular length of wool cloth that was draped according to an exact prescription. Its surface was unbroken, and it required no fastening with pins or buckles.

Wealthy Romans sprinkled gold dust on their hair to obtain the popular fair-haired look.

The Colosseum is the giant amphitheater built in Rome. Unlike earlier amphitheaters, which were nearly all dug into convenient hillsides for extra support, the Colosseum is a freestanding structure of stone and concrete.

The first emperor of Rome was Augustus. During his long reign the Roman world entered an era of wealth, peace, and cultural achievement that became known as the Augustan Age.

Roman numerals are a system for representing numbers with letters of the Latin, or Roman, alphabet. The system dates back about 2,000 years. When a numeral is followed by one of equal or lesser value, their values are added together: II = 2; VI = 6; CLV = 155. A numeral is never used more than three times in a row. Instead, the value is expressed by a smaller numeral followed by a larger numeral. The smaller numeral is subtracted from the larger one. For example, instead of IIII, the number 4 is written as IV (5 - 1).

I = 1
V = 5
X = 10
L = 50
C = 100
D = 500
M = 1,000

Find the Roman Numeral

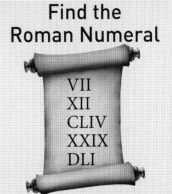

VII
XII
CLIV
XXIX
DLI

ANCIENT AMERICA

The earliest peoples of the Americas are known as Paleo-Indians. They lived by hunting and gathering. As people began to settle down and expand their diets, they developed what are called Archaic cultures. In addition to foraging, Archaic peoples began to experiment with agriculture. By about 2300 BC Indians in the Andes Mountains of South America had adopted a fully agricultural way of life. They began to settle in villages. Farming villages appeared by 2000 BC in Middle America (present-day Mexico and Central America) and somewhat later in Northern America (present-day United States and Canada).

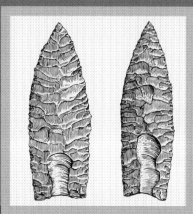

Paleo-Indians shared the land with such large mammals as mammoths, mastodons, and giant bison. The people of the Clovis culture, one of the best-known Paleo-Indian cultures of North America, left behind one of the most distinctive Paleo-Indian artifact types—the Clovis point, which was used for hunting.

The Archaic cultures arose in response to environmental changes. Beginning some 11,500 years ago, temperatures rose dramatically worldwide. Very large animals such as mammoths could not cope with the change and became extinct. Other animals, such as bison, survived by becoming smaller. As the environment changed, so did the Indians' lifestyles. The most visible change was in their diet. Archaic peoples used a wider range of plant and animal foods than the Paleo-Indians had.

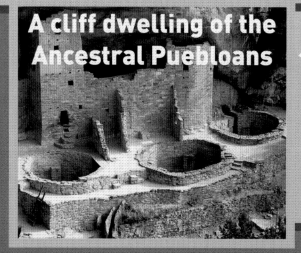

A cliff dwelling of the Ancestral Puebloans

In the first centuries AD three major farming cultures arose in the Southwest: the Ancestral Pueblo (also known as the Anasazi), the Mogollon, and the Hohokam. Indians of the Southwest had begun to grow corn and squash by about 1200 BC.

The first great Indian culture in Middle America was that of the Olmec. They lived on the hot, humid lowland coast of the Gulf of Mexico in what is now southern Mexico. San Lorenzo, the oldest known Olmec center, dates to about 1150 BC. At that time the rest of Middle America had only simple farming villages.

Later Indian cultures in Mexico and Central America showed the influence of the Olmec. In the first millennium AD these civilizations created the first cities in the Western Hemisphere. The Maya of Guatemala and the Yucatán Peninsula built cities with stone temples, pyramids, palaces, ball courts, and plazas.

Mayan ruins in Tulum, Mexico

In the 15th and early 16th centuries, the American Indian people known as the Aztec ruled a large empire in what is now Mexico.

The great civilization of the Incas extended along the Pacific coast of South America from modern Ecuador southward to central Chile and inland across the Andes. The Incas had conquered this vast territory in a single century, and they ruled its people through a highly organized government.

Did the Incas have a writing system?

True or False?

 T F

ANCIENT MONUMENTS AND CITIES

Knossos
What: palace and city
Built by: the Minoan civilization
When: 2500 BC to 1400 BC
Where: the island of Crete, Greece

Palenque
What: city
Built by: the Maya
When: about 600 to 900
Where: Chiapas state, Mexico

Ring for ball games

Uxmal
What: city
Built by: the Maya
When: about 700
Where: Yucatán state, Mexico

Easter Island

What: more than 600 stone statues called *moai*
Built by: Polynesian islanders
When: beginning 700 to 850, ending 1400 to 1600
Where: South Pacific island

Angkor

What: capital city
Built by: the Khmer Empire
When: 9th century to 13th century
Where: north-western Cambodia

Borobudur

What: Buddhist monument
Built by: the Shailendra dynasty
When: between about 778 to 850
Where: Java, Indonesia

The Forbidden City

What: imperial palace complex
Built by: the Ming dynasty
When: first built from 1406 to 1420
Where: Beijing, China

Timbuktu

What: city
Began as: a meeting place for nomads
Became a city: about 1000
Where: Mali, Africa

Find it!

ARCHITECTURE AROUND THE WORLD

In prehistoric times people built simple shelters to protect themselves from inclement weather, predatory animals, and other humans. As time passed and they learned more about building materials and methods, humans began to construct first huts, then castles and cathedrals, and ultimately skyscrapers and factories.

Large areas in the United States Southwest, the Middle East, and North Africa are very dry, with hot days and cool nights most of the year. In these conditions, the Pueblo Indians of the Southwest built homes with thick adobe roofs and walls to provide insulation against heat.

Climate and Building Materials Affect Form

A trullo is a conical, stone-roofed building found in the Apulia region of Italy. On a whitewashed cylindrical wall the builders put circles of gray stone, held in place without mortar by gravity and lateral opposition—that is, leaning against each other.

In traditional Japanese homes, permanent partitions are rare. *Fusuma* may be closed to create separate rooms or opened to convert the entire house into a single room.

Traditional houses in the Arab lands of the Middle East and North Africa have flat roofs where families eat supper and sleep in the cool night air.

In the low mountains and hills of Switzerland, houses have steep gabled roofs that shed rain and snow.

History

Dinosaurs where discoverd by Mary Leckey. When she had discoverd the fossells many people scintests and many others gatherd to talk about this 1 fossle. And thanks to Mary Leckey we can see Musemems filled whith the bones of incretiblle creators. Allso we can do a subject in schoolles to learn more about these creatours. fasanating trips. d takeing field to thise musenums.

Fun fact

Ancient horses used to have 3 toes and were as big a sheep.

1973

Sears Tower (now Willis Tower), Chicago

When was the term *skyscraper* first used?

1931

Empire State Building, New York

1884-1885

first building to use steel girder construction

1860s

1857

steel becomes widely available in the United States

1854

first passenger elevator put into service

848

demonstration of passenger elevator with safety brake

Cast Iron Building, New York

Skyscraper ID

ARCHITECTURAL ACHIEVEMENTS

▲ Lalibela, Ethiopia, is the site of 11 monolithic churches. The churches, designated a UNESCO World Heritage site in 1978, were hewn out of solid rock, entirely below ground level, in a variety of styles.

▲ Each year, the Guggenheim Museum attracts millions of visitors to its locations in several cities, including New York City; Venice, Italy; and Bilbao, Spain. The museum buildings in New York and Bilbao (shown here) have been hailed as architectural masterpieces.

▲ One of the most costly and extravagant buildings in the world, the Palace of Versailles was the principal residence of the French kings and the seat of France's government from 1682 to 1789.

▲ The Hagia Sophia is a cathedral built at Constantinople (now Istanbul, Turkey) in the 6th century under the direction of the Byzantine emperor Justinian I. By general consensus, it is the most important Byzantine structure.

▲ The enormous Todai Temple, in Nara, Japan, is the center of the Kegon sect of Japanese Buddhism. At the center of the complex is the Great Buddha Hall, a huge wooden building that is one of the largest wooden buildings in the world.

▲ New York City's Chrysler Building was designed by William Van Alen and is often cited as the epitome of the **Art Deco** skyscraper.

Brazilian architect Oscar Niemeyer, an early exponent of modern architecture in Latin America, is particularly noted for his work on Brasília, the new capital of Brazil. These buildings are the National Congress buildings.

Which of these other buildings was designed by Oscar Neimeyer?

What bridge is this?

Brooklyn Bridge, New York

Golden Gate Bridge, San Francisco

What bridge is this?

Tower Bridge, London

London Bridge, London

What bridge is this?

Akashi Kaikyo Bridge, Japan

San Francisco–Oakland Bay Bridge, California

WORLD RELIGIONS

The existence of religion is rooted in the fundamental human desire to try to understand the origin of the world, why there is death, or the answers to other basic questions. The word religion comes from the Latin word *religio*, which to the ancient Romans represented all the unknown forces around them that inspired awe and anxiety. Their religion was based on establishing mutual trust between the divine and human in order to secure the benevolence of the gods and their help in mastering those unknown forces.

Monotheistic religions such as Judaism, Christianity, and Islam center on the belief in and worship of one, unique God.

Virtually all other religions—including Buddhism, Hinduism, Daoism, **Shinto**, most of the indigenous religions of Africa and Oceania, and the religions of ancient Greece and Rome—have embraced some form of polytheism, or the belief in more than one deity.

Stained glass window from an Episcopal church in Florida

The beliefs and practices of Christianity are based on the teachings of Jesus Christ. Christianity is divided into three main denominations: Roman Catholic, Eastern Orthodox, and Protestant. There are more Christians in the world (some 2 billion at the beginning of the 21st century) than followers of any other single religion.

Along with Christianity and Islam, Judaism is one of the three major monotheistic religions of the world. Of the three, Judaism is the oldest.

A Jewish synagogue in Tbilisi, Georgia

According to biblical tradition, the origins of the faith can be traced back at least 3,000 years to Abraham, the patriarch who is considered the father of the Jewish faith, and his descendants who formed the nation of Israel.

Muslim pilgrims visit the shrine of Kaaba in Mecca.

A major world religion, Islam is based on the revelations of the Prophet Muhammad and was first established in Mecca (now in Saudi Arabia). Altogether there are more than 1 billion Muslims around the world.

Buddhist temple in Myanmar

Buddhism is the name for a complex system of beliefs developed around the teachings of the Buddha. Though used by many religious groups in ancient India, the title Buddha (meaning "the Enlightened One") became associated with the founder of Buddhism, Siddhartha Gautama, who lived between the 6th and the 4th centuries BC.

What is animism?

A Hindu temple in Sri Lanka

The major religion of the Indian subcontinent is Hinduism. One of the oldest of the world's religions, Hinduism dates back more than 3,000 years, though its present forms are of more recent origin. In the early 21st century, more than 90 percent of the world's Hindus lived in India, and the religion had nearly one billion adherents worldwide.

A Daoist temple in China

Daoism is a philosophical and religious tradition that developed in China in ancient times. Daoist philosophy speaks of a universal Dao, which is nameless and unknowable, the essential unifying element of all that is.

What do you know?

Judaism	Hinduism
Christianity	Daoism
Islam	Shinto
Buddhism	Animism

HOLIDAYS

Festivals and holidays have been celebrated since ancient times. The earliest festivals seem to have been connected with offerings to the dead. Later, people celebrated the change of seasons with festivals. Many modern festivals and holidays originated in religious celebrations. Holidays celebrating historic events and other occasions developed later.

Celebrating a New Year

Celebrating the end of one year and the start of a new one is an age-old religious, social, and cultural observance in all parts of the world. The earliest known record of a New Year festival dates from 2000 BC in Mesopotamia.

Fireworks over Sydney, Australia, on New Year's Eve

Lunar New Year

Apples and honey for Rosh Hashana

Lights for Diwali, the festival of lights

Fasts and Feasts

The Western religions of Judaism, Christianity, and Islam have, from their inception, set aside certain times in the year for regular fasting observances. The forgoing of food and drink may be partial or total and may last for a short or long period of time.

Easter eggs

Food for an evening meal during the month of Ramadan

National Holidays

Many countries have national holidays. Tradition or law has established certain days for the whole country to celebrate.

What holiday is celebrated in Texas and other American states on June 19?

Dancers at a Cinco de Mayo festival

Parades celebrate July 4 in America

True or False?   T   F

MUSIC AROUND THE WORLD

All ancient civilizations entered historical times with a flourishing musical culture. That the earliest writers explained it in terms of legend and myth is evidence of the remote beginnings of the art of sound. During humankind's long history, music has been sung and played in countless ways. Each culture developed its own style of singing and its own instruments.

Every African community has its own music. The traditional music created by Africa's many peoples has always formed an important part of everyday life on the continent. In more recent times, African popular music has blended traditional styles with elements taken from American music. In turn, African music has had a great impact on music far beyond Africa's borders.

In India, music has been put into the service of religion from earliest times. Vedic chant is the expression of hymns from the Vedas, the ancient scriptures of Hinduism.

The arts of music and dance are often intertwined in Oceanic cultures. Music and dance in Polynesia and Micronesia are audible and visual extensions of poetry, whereas in Melanesia they are aimed more at spectacular display during times of life crises and as a part of secret-society rituals.

When a single vocalist sounds more than one pitch simultaneously, it is called throat-singing. Throat-singing originated among the indigenous Turko-Mongol tribes of southern Siberia and western Mongolia.

Chinese writings claim that in 2697 BC the emperor Huangdi sent a scholar, Ling Lun, to the western mountain area to cut bamboo pipes that could emit sounds matching the call of the *fenghuang*. The *fenghuang* was an immortal bird whose rare appearance signaled harmony in the reign of a new emperor.

Native American performances integrate music, dance, spirituality, and social communion in multilayered events. Each performance occasion has its own musical styles and genres.

Western cultures generally share the same genres of folk music. One of the most important is the ballad, generally a short narrative song with repeated lines. Epics are longer narratives in heroic style, which sometimes require many hours to sing. Some songs are ceremonial, meant to accompany events in the human life cycle or in the community's year. These women sing a traditional Ukrainian song.

Music Facts   Yes   No

MUSICAL INSTRUMENTS

An object that can be used to produce music is called a musical instrument. A musical instrument may be as large and complicated as a pipe organ or as small and simple as a tiny bell or whistle. Musical instruments can be grouped according to how the sound is produced. The main categories are percussion, stringed, wind, keyboard, and electronic.

▼ Talking drums from West Africa can be heard over a distance of 20 miles (32 kilometers).

The timpani, or kettledrums, are of Eastern origin. Small Arabian kettledrums were introduced into Europe as early as the 13th century. ▶

Evidence suggests that cymbals originated in the region of modern-day Turkey or in India. They were used in rituals in a number of ancient cultures, including those of Assyria, Israel, and Egypt. ▼

The koto is a Japanese 13-stringed board **zither** with movable bridges.

The balalaika is a Russian stringed musical instrument similar to a guitar.

The banjo is a stringed musical instrument of African origin. It was popularized in the United States by slaves in the 19th century and then exported to Europe.

A member of the wind instrument family, the bagpipe is one of the oldest reed instruments—it was known to the civilizations of ancient Greece, Rome, and Persia.

The first saxophone was patented by Antoine-Joseph Sax in Paris, France, in 1846.

When was the first electronic instrument created?

SPORTS AROUND THE WORLD

No one can say exactly when sports began. Since ancient times people have engaged in footraces, wrestled, and hunted for sport. Archaeological evidence indicates that ball games were common among ancient peoples in many parts of the world. After ancient times people continued to play sports, but they were usually unorganized. Organized sports became more common in the 1700s and 1800s.

▲
In some ancient cultures sports were a part of religious practices. The most famous association of sports and religion was certainly the Olympic Games, which Greek tradition dates from 776 BC.

Nicknamed "Lightning Bolt," Jamaican sprinter Usain Bolt electrified track-and-field fans around the world with his gold medal victories in the 100- and 200-meter races at both the 2008 Olympic Games in Beijing, China, and the 2012 Olympic Games in London, England. ▼

Sport parachuting, or skydiving, began in 1914 with the first free fall, a jump made with a delayed opening of the parachute.

How old is the sport of ice skating?

It was invented in 1750.

It developed about 500 years ago.

It is at least 1,000 years old.

he game of soccer, or association football, as it is properly
alled, is the world's most popular team sport. Virtually
very country on Earth plays the game.

Where and when was **soccer** first played?

What was the oldest organized sport in North America?

rugby

lacrosse

basketball

**Skiing was a prehistoric activity; the oldest known skis are
about 8,000 years old and were discovered in Russia.**

Sports Trivia

Where was volleyball first played?
France
India
United States

A   B

THE HISTORY OF MONEY

If a society's economy is to function efficiently, there must be some standard by which to measure the value of all goods and services. For many centuries in most societies this standard has been money. In the modern world money appears in two forms, paper and metal. Historically the metal has been mostly in flat, round pieces called coins.

Cowrie shells

Anything can serve as money, from the wampum (beads made from shells) of American Indians, to whales' teeth among the Fijians, to large stone disks on the Pacific island of Yap.

4,000 years ago: Money is invented.

7th century BC: Coins are invented.

This coin dates back to 566 BC.

Who is a numismatist?

Coin ID

Ever since money came into use in the ancient world, there has been counterfeiting. Early money was in the form of coins with a specific content of gold, silver, or other metal. Making counterfeit coins was relatively easy. A metal of equal weight could be gold- or silver-plated and passed on to the public as genuine.

Philadelphia mint

1792: The Philadelphia mint is established in the United States.

Middle Ages: Paper money originates in the West.

About 1200: Paper money is widely used in China.

Functions performed by banks today have been carried out by individuals, families, or state officials for at least 4,000 years. Clay tablets dating from about 2000 BC indicate that the Babylonians deposited personal valuables for a service charge of one 60th of their worth.

MORE ABOUT MONEY

Current Currency

Which of these currencies are used today?

- bolívar
- deutsche mark
- drachma
- lira

deutsche mark

quetzal

- naira
- pound sterling
- quetzal
- ruble

On the Dollar

- Benjamin Franklin
- Alexander Hamilton
- Thomas Jefferson
- Abraham Lincoln

Dollar Signs

The name *dollar* is derived from that of a silver coin first minted in 1519 in St. Joachimsthal, Bohemia, which became known as a Joachimsthaler. This name was changed to thaler, or taler, in Germany; to dalder, or daler, in the Netherlands; and to dollar in Great Britain.

When did the United States start using paper money?

These are dollar bills. If they don't look familiar, it's because they're Australian dollars!

Who's Who

INVENTIONS IN HISTORY

Invention began in prehistory. Long centuries before the invention of writing, early humans had worked out many important tools. Among these were fire-making devices, the wheel and axle, the pulley, the saw, the screw, the wedge, and the inclined plane.

In very ancient times, man covered his feet with the closest available materials—bark, woven grass, leaves, or animal skins. He held these crude coverings to his feet with thongs.

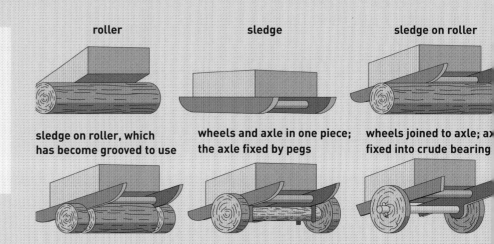

roller

sledge

sledge on roller

sledge on roller, which has become grooved to use

wheels and axle in one piece; the axle fixed by pegs

wheels joined to axle; ax fixed into crude bearing

▲ No one knows when the wheel was invented or who invented it, but the wheel was evidently the result of long development. A Sumerian pictograph, dated about 3500 BC, shows a sledge equipped with wheels.

The ancestor of the plow is the prehistoric digging stick. The earliest plows were probably digging sticks fashioned with handles for pulling or pushing.

During the Han dynasty (206 BC to AD 220), China made many advancements in science, mathematics, and technology that were unknown in the Western world. Chinese inventions of the period included paper, water clocks, sundials, locks for controlling water levels in streams, a seismograph for measuring the strength of earthquakes, and compasses.

Researchers have found evidence of archery that leads many of them to believe that it originated in more than one place. Other evidence has been found that shows the use of bows and arrows by peoples in every part of the world except Australia.

German craftsman Johannes Gutenberg (1395?–1468) is believed to have developed the first printing press. He did not actually invent printing, nor did he print the first book. However, his press made printing practical, and his method of using movable metal type endured almost unchanged for five centuries.

True or False?
T   F

INVENTIONS ALL AROUND

The world's progress is due largely to inventions. Whenever a new method, machine, or gadget is invented, it helps humankind to live a little easier or better or longer.

The idea of a slide fastener was exhibited by Whitcomb L. Judson at the World's Columbian Exposition of 1893 in Chicago, Illinois. ▼

German engineer Carl von Linde (1842–1934) invented a continuous process of liquefying gases in large quantities that formed a basis for the modern technology of refrigeration.

Margaret E. Knight (1838–1914) invented an attachment for paper-bag-folding machines that allowed the production of square-bottomed bags. ▼

U.S. inventor Charles Goodyear (1800–60) invented the vulcanization process tha made possible the commerci use of rubber. ▼

Pen and Ink History

Writing inks date from about:

2500 BC

100 AD

In 1772 the first patent was issued in England for this:

making colored ink

using a mixture of a soluble iron salt with an extract of tannin for blue-black ink

The quill pen was invented by:

the Greeks

the Romans

When was the fountain pen developed?

1660s

1880s

The ancient Egyptians used these to write:

brushes made from reeds

an iron or wooden stick, called a stylus

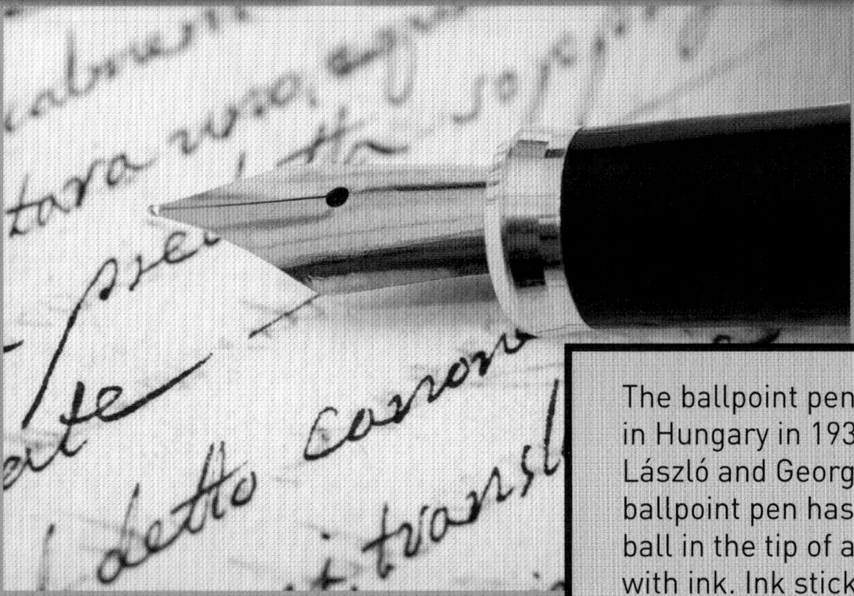

◀**fountain pen**

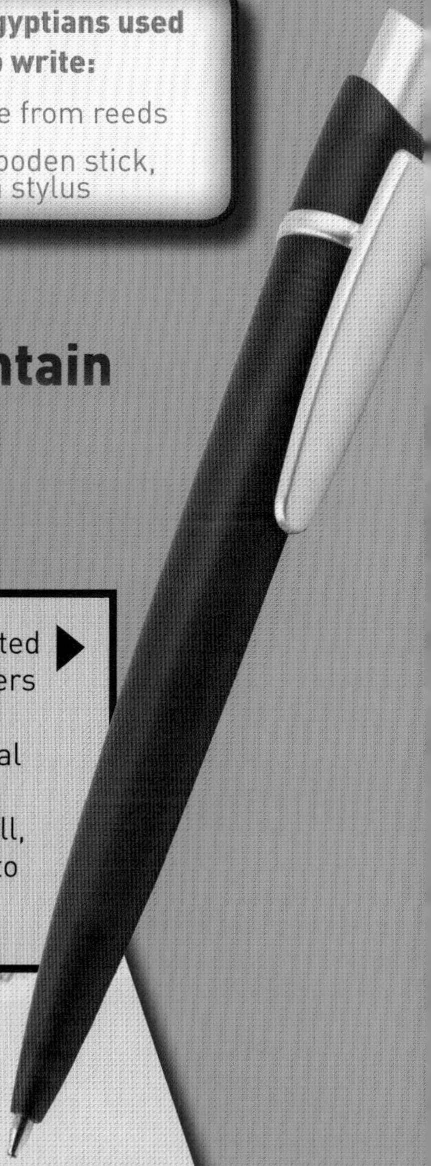

The ballpoint pen was invented ▶ in Hungary in 1935 by brothers László and Georg Bíró. The ballpoint pen has a tiny metal ball in the tip of a tube filled with ink. Ink sticks to the ball, and the ball rolls the ink onto the paper.

A patent is a right of ownership, usually of an invention. The invention itself is not owned by a patent; the right to use, manufacture, and sell it is. ▼

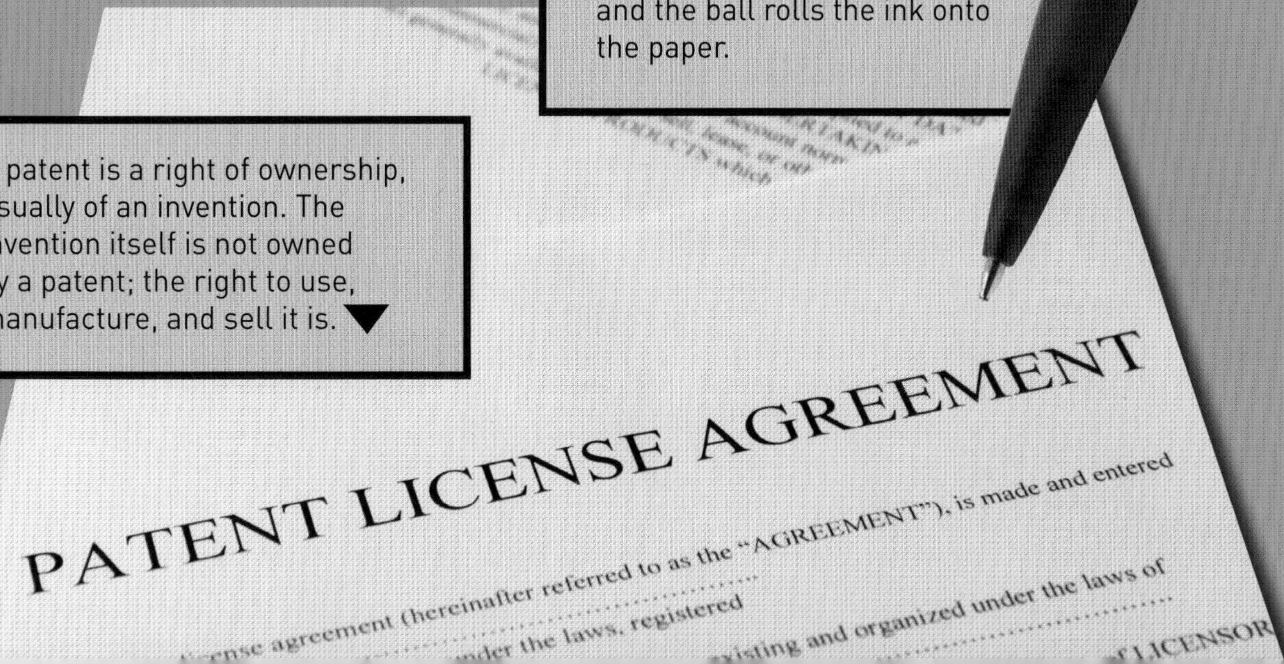

PATENT LICENSE AGREEMENT

PLANTS AROUND THE WORLD

Wherever there is sunlight, air, and soil, plants can be found. To date, more than 300,000 plant species have been identified and described. However, **botanists** estimate that there are tens of thousands of unidentified species yet to be discovered, especially in less explored ecosystems such as tropical forests.

The First Plants

The first plants appeared on land more than 400 million years ago.

moss

liverwort

fern

buttercup

At least 250,000 species of flowering plants are known. All of them descend from a primitive ancestor that no longer exists.

The first botanist?

Humans and Plants

Humans are dependent upon plants. Directly or indirectly, plants provide food, clothing, fuel, shelter, and many other necessities of life.

palm

wheat

flax

aloe

fruit

When did humans first domesticate plants?

Seasoning Quiz

EXTREME DANGEROUS AND WEIRD

The oldest living trees on Earth are thought to be the bristlecone pines. Representatives grow in Colorado, Utah, Nevada, and Arizona.

Giant sequoias are among the oldest of the forest trees, living for 3,000 years or more. The giant sequoia reaches heights of more than 280 feet (85 meters) and may have a maximum trunk diameter of more than 25 feet (8 meters).

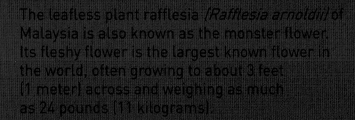

The leafless plant rafflesia *(Rafflesia arnoldii)* of Malaysia is also known as the monster flower. Its fleshy flower is the largest known flower in the world, often growing to about 3 feet (1 meter) across and weighing as much as 24 pounds (11 kilograms).

Moss grows on a boat in Antartica.

In Antarctica, the most common plants are lichens, which comprise about 350 species. Mosses and liverworts grow mostly in ice-free areas along the coast.

Among the most [...]
cacti is the night-[...]

Does the American aloe, also known as the century plant, only bloom once a century?
▼

◀ **Pitcher plant**

Most plants get the nut[...]
they need from soil. So[...]
also get nutrients by ca[...]
digesting insects. For th[...]
they are called carnivor[...]

▲ **Foxglove**
(Digitalis purpurea)

Though there are some 250,000 species of flowering plants, only

Plant

NATURE IN DANGER

Deforestation

Deforestation is the clearing, or cutting down, of forests. The word is normally used to describe the actions of humans in removing forests from the planet, rather than destruction caused by such natural events as hurricanes. In recent times, the number of forests being lost through deforestation has grown enormously.

Desertification

The spread or encroachment of a desert environment into a nondesert region is a process known as desertification. This process results from a number of factors, including changes in climate and the influence of human activities. Desertification drains an arid or semiarid land of its life-supporting capabilities. The process of desertification is extremely difficult to reverse.

Pollution

Much of the world's air, water, and land is now partially poisoned by chemical wastes. Some places have become uninhabitable. This pollution exposes people all around the globe to new risks from disease. Many species of plants and animals have become endangered or are now extinct. As a result of these developments, governments have passed laws to limit or reverse the threat of environmental pollution.

Loss of biodiversity

Exotic plants brought into Australia are a major threat to native species. Among the exotic weeds are wild turnip, shown here, which competes with crops as well as native plants.

As living things evolve, some species become extinct, or die out completely. Extinction is a natural phenomenon. It is clear, however, that humans have been greatly accelerating this process, especially since the mid-20th century. Scientists estimate that human activities have been causing species to become extinct at hundreds to perhaps a thousand times the background, or natural, rate. The genetic diversity within species, especially domesticated animals and crops, has also decreased.

True or False?   T   F

THE PLANETS

The planets that orbit the Sun are part of the solar system, which includes the Sun and all the bodies that circle it. The Sun governs the planets' orbital motions by gravitational attraction and provides the planets with light and heat.

◀ Exploration of the planet Venus with spacecraft began in the 1960s. More than 20 unmanned spacecraft have visited Venus.

How many of the planets can be seen without a telescope?

Relatively little was ▶ known about Mercury until the Mariner 10 spacecraft visited it in 1974–75. During that flight, more than 2,300 images were taken, including this one.

The solar system's four inner planets are much smaller than its four outer planets, and all eight are dwarfed by the Sun they orbit.

How many Earths would fit inside Jupiter?

Sun
865,000 mi
(1,392,000 km)

Jupiter
89,000 mi
(143,000 km)

Saturn
74,900 mi
(120,600 km)

Neptune
31,000 mi
(50,000 km)

Venus
7,500 mi
(12,100 km)

Mars
4,200 mi
(6,800 km)

Mercury
3,000 mi
(4,900 km)

Earth
7,940 mi
(12,780 km)

Uranus
32,000 mi
(51,000 km)

Did you know? A B

◀ Jupiter's moon Io

The first three spacecraft missions to Jupiter—named Pioneer, Voyager, and Galileo—dramatically increased scientists' knowledge about the giant planet in the late 20th century.

The first craft to fly successfully by Mars was Mariner 4, which photographed the planet as it passed by in July 1965.

Four unmanned spacecraft have visited Saturn, obtaining images and data that have greatly increased knowledge about the planet.

Voyager 2 became the first—and so far only—spacecraft to encounter Uranus, in January 1986, and Neptune, in August 1989. This image shows Uranus's nine rings.

When was Pluto considered a planet?

Relatively little was known about Neptune until the Voyager 2 spacecraft—the only mission to the distant planet—flew by it in 1989.

THE SOLAR SYSTEM

As the Sun rushes through space at a speed of roughly 150 miles (240 kilometers) per second, it takes many smaller objects along with it. These include the planets and dwarf planets; their moons; and small bodies such as asteroids, comets, and meteoroids. The solar system is, of course, not alone in space. The Sun is a star like countless others, and other stars also have planets circling them. The Sun is part of the Milky Way galaxy, a huge group of stars swirling around in a pinwheel shape.

Are there planets outside our solar system?

yes

no

A comet is a small chunk of dust and ice that orbits the Sun. There are billions of comets in the solar system, but most never pass close by Earth.

Ceres' layers

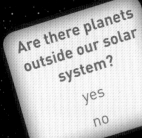

Thin, dusty outer crust

Rocky inner core

Water-ice layer

Could an asteroid collide with Earth?

Asteroids are small, rocky bodies that orbit, or travel around, the Sun. In general, they are materials left over from when the planets formed. Ceres is the largest asteroid by far, with a diameter of about 584 miles, or 940 kilometers. It is massive enough to also be considered a dwarf planet.

What is the difference between a meteor and a meteorite?

A meteoroid is a chunk of rock or metal from space that falls through the atmosphere, or layer of gases, surrounding Earth. Most meteoroids burn up in the atmosphere.

Find It!

Sometimes an unusually large number of small meteors can be seen in rapid succession—perhaps more than 50 per hour. Such a display is called a meteor shower and occurs when the Earth passes through a swarm of meteoroids.

Sun

How many galaxies are there?

millions

billions

How big is the Milky Way galaxy?

1,000 light years

150,000 light years

1 billion light years

A cloud of gas and dust that occurs in the space between the stars is known as a nebula. Some nebulae give birth to new stars, and dying stars expel nebulae.

WHAT HAPPENED HERE?

What happened first?

the building of the Empire State Building

Mariner 10's visit to Mercury

What happened first?

the widespread use of paper money in China

the printing of the Gutenberg Bible

What happened first?

the use of writing in ancient Egypt

the use of skis in what is now Russia

What sport was invented in Massachusetts in 1895?

volleyball

basketball

The saxophone was patented during this decade.

the 1740s

the 1840s

Uxmal was built by the Maya during this century.

the 700s

the 1400s

What happened in Babylon in the late 18th century BC?

the development of Hammurabi's code

Buddhism began to develop

The first mammals appeared during this period.

the Triassic period

the Jurassic period

the Cretaceous period

What was demonstrated at a 1893 Exposition in Chicago, Illinois?

the slide fastener (later called a zipper)

a passenger elevator with safety brake